BEYOND THE FOREST

The Story of Parsifal
and the Grail

Kelvin Hall

Hawthorn Press

Published by Hawthorn Press, Hawthorn House, 1 Lansdown Lane, Stroud, Gloucestershire, GL5 1BJ, UK
Tel: (01453) 757040 Fax: (01453) 751138
www.hawthornpress.com

Cover design by Patrick Roe, Southgate Solutions Ltd.
Cover illustration by Anthony Hodge.
Typesetting by Hawthorn Press, Stroud, Glos.
Printed in the UK by Cromwell Press, Trowbridge, Wilts.

British Library Cataloguing in Publication Data applied for.

ISBN 1 869 890 73 6

Contents

Thanks

The encouragement and valued comments of a number of people contributed to the final form of this tale. Martin Large first suggested the idea. Aonghus Gordon, as so often, provided a home for the first tellings.

The following were among those who took time to voice their reactions:

Gabriel Millar, Adrian Luyk, Michael Moran, Karin Jarman, Liz Taylor, June Peters, Fiona Collins, Katie Zienko, Martin Hardiman, Phillipa Williams-Brett, Adrian Locher, Hugh Lupton, John Meletiou, Cheryl Sanders. My wife Barbara first told me the story, thus opening the door on many years of perilous and greatly rewarded adventures.

Foreword

Kelvin Hall's rendering of the 'Parsifal' legend is a welcome addition to the texts available for teachers in Steiner (Waldorf) schools. Crafted by an experienced and capable story-teller, it conveys the spirit and essential content of this great epic in a style easily accessible to the modern reader.

Rudolf Steiner was keen that the oldest pupils in Waldorf schools should have the opportunity to experience the powerful themes of this mediaeval story. He saw the moral journey of the youthful hero, Parsifal, as one all modern young people can connect strongly with. Over-protected by his mother, naive, yet wilful and instinctive, he wins through to a stage of self-realisation and moral certitude only through a process of endless mistakes and confusions. His journey is one of self-actualisation through suffering and the recognition of suffering in others. His ultimate assumption of moral responsibility becomes a healing deed for the future and provides a picture with which the modern young person can identify and work strongly.

John Burnett

Introduction

Why should anyone be interested in a new version of an ancient story in which a bunch of men in iron suits try their hardest to knock each other senseless, while an array of impossibly beautiful women float around in various tragic moods, being assaulted, neglected or adored? Why have a succession of modern writers seized on the Medieval Grail legend to find insights into predicaments facing contemporary men and women?

The Grail, according to Edward Whitmont, 'is the most significant and most modern form of the redemption myth.'[1] Robert Johnson bases his book on male psychology[2] on one of the versions, using it as a guide to patterns of thought and feeling found perennially in men. Joseph Campbell called it 'the first sheerly individualistic mythology of the human race.'[3] The tale is a continuous undercurrent in the work of Rudolf Steiner and his students for whom it contains the secrets of the modern initiation path. In Steiner-Waldorf schools it is used for pupils who have reached sixteen, for its graphic portrayal of the young person struggling to find the path that is right for them.

The unfolding of the narrative eludes neat definitions. 'There is no one Grail,' writes A.T. Hatto,[4] 'just as there is no one Grail story.' He was referring to the intriguingly differing versions which have come down to us, but he could equally have been alluding to the way that the narrative leads us into a maze of twists, turns and successive layers of reality which defy our habitual expectations. This is particularly true of the von Eschenbach version I follow here. We think we have grasped it, then find otherwise. Thankfully, the tale has in it something to challenge every brand of fundamentalism, whether Christian, Pagan, Feminist, Patriarchal or New Age.

There is plenty that could alienate a modern audience. The aristocratic milieu, for instance, may seem politically suspect. Unless, that is, we see that most of us have a potential realm of activity in which we are sovereign like the nobles of the tale. Like them, we may have battles to fight which call on our courage, judgement and skill, and which we can lose through our own unwitting self-sabotage.

The tale may present greater difficulties in the portrayal of women. Herzeloyde, Sigune, Jeschute and Condwiramurs present mainly passive figures which might seem undermining or misleading to contemporary men and women. It is more profitable, however, to see them not as models of behaviour, but as moods or aspects of feeling which can be encountered at times in any age, setting, or in each of us. Many women enthusiasts for the tale have said that, in any case, they identify most readily with Parsifal himself, the aspirant trying to make sense of a world full of pitfalls.

In fact, the tale is rich with images which resonate down the centuries, as raw and as brilliant as if they had just appeared. It begins with a single parent, dismayed, like many today, over the question 'How should I bring up my boy? Does he have to be infected by the cult of aggression and conquest which characterises contemporary male culture?' She then, like so many in this age, tries to withdraw to a place protected from harmful influences.

But of course, when the boy first casts his totally innocent eyes upon warriors in all their glory he is instantly hooked. He is overwhelmed by a fascination undiluted by knowledge. Likewise, when he finds himself for the first time alone with a lovely woman he is even more awkward and clumsy than most of us, climbing straight into her bed without the slightest knowledge of implications, conventions or boundaries. He goes on to engage fully in the world of bloody competition, triumph, fame and disaster. He is armoured and carries weapons of death. Can he do this and still give voice to his soul?

Trying to make sense of the world and his place in it, his progress consists of effortless successes, when he follows his natural talents, then appalling blunders which occur when he tries his hardest to follow instructions. He meets Anfortas, the Grail King, terribly stricken in his maleness firstly by his vulnerability to feminine allure, secondly by the wound which disables him and casts a shadow over his land and people. Many a man struggling with today's inner conflicts – the impact of feminism, convulsions in family life and workplace, awareness of a blighted planet – might feel very similar.

The tale proceeds, interweaving the extreme polarities of human experience. Ultimately, it seems, Parsifal fuses impossible opposites. He seeks glory, but also receives the ultimate grace. He is a conqueror and a healer. He unites erotic and marital happiness. How can this be possible? Here we touch on mysteries, which facile explanations cannot illumine. The story gives clues, and only in the telling, the listening and the living can we find our own way to the Castle.

My aim in this volume is neither psychological interpretation nor academic research. I am a storyteller. Wolfram von Eschenbach's 13th-century rendition of the Parsifal legend is held by many to be the most complete and subtle – though all the versions, including the Welsh Peredur and the French Perceval have their merits and their champions. I have tried to honour Wolfram's treatment and would claim to have added no major incident or detail, though a number are omitted. I look for what gives this tale momentum. What grips us? What really speaks to me, and hopefully my audience too? In the end, therefore, the voice is my own.

Live storytelling has revived throughout the world in the last decade and more. Its code of honour, agreed between most tellers, is that we can steal stories from each other, but tell them in our own language and style. Different tellings draw out all the immeasurable riches hidden in each old story. This was, after all, precisely what Shakespeare, Chaucer and Homer did. It is in such a spirit that this version, albeit on the printed page, is offered. In fact it grew out of live tellings, first at Ruskin Mill in Nailsworth in 1997, then all over Britain, and the response and comments of audiences have been crucial to its development. It is offered only as one version of many existing, and many still to come.

Kelvin Hall   Michaelmas Day 1999

1. Edward C. Whitmont, *Return of the Goddess.*
   Routledge & Kegan, Paul, 1983.

2. Robert Johnson, *HE.*
   Harper & Row, 1989.

3. Joseph Campbell, *The Masks of God,* Vol 4.
   Arkana, 1983.

4. Wolfram von Eschenbach, *Parzifal.*
   trans. A.T. Hatto, Penguin Classics, 1980.

THE NAMES

HERZELOYDE   (sometimes known as 'Heart's Sorrow'). Married to Gahmuret, mother of Parsifal.

GAHMURET   Utterly devoted to warfare and jousting, father of Parsifal.

PARSIFAL   A natural fighter, who grows up in seclusion. Heir to considerable lands, sometimes regarded by translators of von Eschenbach as 'the Welshman'.

JESCHUTE   Wife of the Duke Orilus, surprised by Parsifal while sleeping in her tent.

ORILUS   A powerful Duke who fights Parsifal.

SIGUNE   Cousin of Parsifal, grieving for slain knight.

ITHER   The Red Knight in dispute with Arthur.

ARTHUR   King of Britain, head of the Round Table brotherhood.

KEIE   A knight, Arthur's seneschal or steward.

CUNNEWARE   A noblewoman in Arthur's Hall, who never laughs.

ANTENOR — A dumb jester in Arthur's Hall.

GURNEMANZ — A old knight and tutor of young warriors.

LIAZE — Daughter of Gurnemanz. Attracted to Parsifal.

CONDWIRAMURS — Young Queen of Belrepeire. Beloved of Parsifal.

CLAMIDE — King who besieges Condwiramurs.

ANFORTAS — The wounded Grail King sometimes known as the Fisher King.

REPANSE de SCHOYE — The young woman who carries the Grail in procession.

SEGRAMORS — A keen young knight.

GAWAIN — An accomplished knight, nephew of Arthur.

CUNDRIE — A Sorceress of grotesque appearance.

KINGRIMURSEL — A champion who challenges Gawain on behalf of Vergulaht, his King.

VERGULAHT — A King who feuds with Gawain.

ANTIKONE — Sister of Vergulaht, much attracted to Gawain.

LYPPAUT — A Duke besieged by King Meljanz.

OBIE	Elder daughter of Lyppaut. Beloved of Meljanz, whom she initially spurns.
OBILOT	Younger daughter of Lyppaut. Asks Gawain to be her knight.
MELJANZ	Overlord of Lyppaut, initially rejected by his daughter.
ORGELUSE	Beloved of Gawain.
MALCREATURE	Grotesque page of Orgeluse, brother of Cundrie, the Sorceress, mocker of Gawain.
URIAN	A knight of Arthur accused of rape, hostile to Gawain.
CLINSCHOR	An immensely powerful Sorcerer who created the Castle of Wonders.
ARNIVE	The mother of Arthur. One of those imprisoned in Clinschor's Castle.
ITONJE	Sister of Gawain. Beloved of his enemy, Gramoflanz.
GRAMOFLANZ	Formidable warrior engaged in a blood-feud with Gawain.
FEIREFIZ	Half-brother to Parsifal, ruler of rich lands in North Africa.
BELACANE	A Moorish Queen, first consort of Parsifal's father, Gahmuret.

I: Fool

The silence is broken by hoofbeats, rapidly pounding the floor of the forest. A mud-spattered messenger comes to a castle of grey stone. He rushes up the stairs to a chamber where a woman waits, heavy with child. When she has heard his words she sinks to the ground, felled by shock.

The woman, Herzeloyde, has just been told that her husband, Gahmuret, has been killed in a far-off land. The thrill of battle and tournament had been his ruling passion, something he could never put aside. This outcome was what she had always dreaded. The night before, she had dreamed that she was borne upwards by a fiery star which scattered sparks of lightning about her, that a dragon had torn its way out of her womb and then scuttled off into the distance, never to be seen again.

Three days later she gave birth to a boy-child. Her women cooed over it, and admired the tender shoot between its legs, but she thought,

'What if he grows up like his father, like all men, always thirsting for glory and conquest? Then my heart would be broken a second time. Could there be some way to prevent this? What if I were to take a small band of my people and go to some hidden corner of my lands, and make sure that my son never sees or hears of knights, jousting or warfare?'

So she fled to a remote homestead hidden from the rest of the world by the dense forest called Soltane.
'He must not hear a single word about knights or their weapons,' she commanded her servants. She didn't know that, although this was her only son, he was not

the only son of her husband Gahmuret, who had wandered far across the world in the years before his marriage. This we shall have cause to remember.

The boy grew, running wild in the woods, keen of eye, strong of arm, but soft-hearted. Often, he followed the huntsmen upon whom they all relied for food. Their swiftness and skill enthralled him. Very soon he had fashioned his own bow and arrow. Creeping noiselessly along the edge of a field with bow in hand, he saw a lark hovering above. Swept along by the thrill of it, he aimed and loosed his arrow. The suddenly silent bird plummeted with a soft thud into the furrows. But as soon as he held the ruffled body in his hands, the boy burst into tears of remorse.

A few days later, Herzeloyde watched as he listened transfixed by the chorus of bird song all around them. She saw the tears well up in his eyes. She could not bear to see this tenderness, knowing how easily it could lead to pain. Hastening away, she called for some of her foresters, who came before her in their tunics of green and dun.

'The birds are upsetting my son,' she said, 'you must rid the forest of them!' But soon after, her son ran to her dismayed.

'Our men are hunting the birds! What harm have they done?'

As soon as she heard these words she glimpsed her folly and sighed with a weary smile,

'If God has given the birds their song, then who am I to take it away?' The boy fixed her with his gaze.

'Who is this God person you talk of?' he demanded.

'Well, my beautiful son,' she responded, faltering for an answer, 'he... he's more splendid than any of us, and he gives us help when we need it...' These words the boy took away with him and pondered long. Passing his days thus, he grew towards young manhood, though still seeming more of a child than do most children.

Until the day when, as he wandered among the trees, he felt the ground tremble to the sound of hoofbeats. He looked up and saw God coming towards him along the track. Or several Gods rather, for there were four of them. Such they must be, for never had he seen anyone as splendid, and this was the word his mother had used to describe God. Mighty horses they rode, and wore burnished steel and cloth of the brightest colours. Their mounts snorted as they were pulled to a sudden halt. The sun flashed on the metal-clad limbs of the riders.

'Out of my way, idiot!' yelled one as the young man stood there open-mouthed.

'Come on then, God', demanded the latter, still remembering his mother's tuition '...give me some help!'

'We're not God,' responded another, kinder than the first. 'We're **knights**.' The youth lingeringly caressed the pommel of the man's sword and avidly eyed every inch of his apparel. Then eagerly he asked,

'How could I become a knight?'

'Well,' said the other, humouring him, 'you'd have to go to Arthur, the King, and ask him to make you one. Who knows, maybe he will. You certainly have the looks to appeal to the ladies. But we must go now, for we pursue two others who are called knights, but act like filth.

They've taken a young woman by force.' He wheeled his
great horse round, and in a shower of clods and pebbles
the four were gone.

That night the youth sought out his mother,
'I'm going to become a knight!' he declared. 'I'm going
to Arthur, the King, so he can make me one.'
Herzeloyde recognised the look of iron resolve in his
eyes. Once more, just as she had done when she heard
of Gahmuret's death, she sank to the ground as if a
blade had pierced her through.

When she revived a little, though, her thoughts raced,

'He really means it. I can read it in his eyes, I am not
going to be able to stop him. But can I make sure that
his efforts come to nothing? Yes, if I persuade him to
wear such ridiculous garb that no one will take seriously
his claim to knighthood.'

So she sought him out next morning.
'Here, dear son,' she said, 'I've made you special clothes
for the journey.' She handed him a one-piece suit of
sacking, cut short at the knees and elbows, and a pair of
rough, clumpish boots; to ride, she offered him a sway-
backed and decrepit old pony. He ferreted around in the
sheds where the huntsmen kept their tackle, until he
found the nearest thing to a lance, which was a javelin,
old but light.

But when she saw him thus arrayed, she was even more
fearful.
'Perhaps I can arrange it,' she thought desperately, 'so
that instead of falling into danger out there, he might
meet people who would cherish him and care for him.
Perhaps I can give him advice that will help him to find
them.' She turned to face him. 'Listen, beloved son,' she

said to him earnestly, 'if, on your journey, you meet a man grey in the years of his head, who is willing to be your teacher, then listen to all he says, for such a man will surely be wise. As for women, if you find one who wants your arms around her, and lets you have her ring, then do not hesitate one moment to take it, for you have discovered the greatest treasure in the world.'

Then she watched him ride away. 'Make sure you greet everyone politely!' she called in a last effort to prepare him.

'I will, mother,' came the faint reply. As he vanished into the trees, she felt she had lost everything she ever had in this life.

★ ★ ★ ★ ★

As the mist rose the next morning and golden vapour swirled through the forest, he crossed a stream and came to a place where an exquisitely fashioned tent was pitched. Scarlet, lilac and purple it was coloured, and the tassels which hung around it danced in a light breeze.

The young man slid from his pony wide-eyed and, pulling aside the tent flap, stepped in. Whatever wonders he had seen in his short life were nothing compared with what he now looked upon. He saw a torrent of soft rich hair which all but drowned the pillow over which it tumbled. He saw eyelids closed in sleep, tender lips parted a little. Flesh soft, warm and still, save for the slight rise and fall of the breasts. A bedcover which in the heat had been pushed down to the curve of the hips. A gleaming ring about a slender finger. He looked, though he did not know it, upon Jeschute, the lovely wife of the Duke Orilus, who had just lately ridden from that spot.

The youth devotedly followed the words of advice with which his mother had bade him farewell. Without hesitation he clambered onto the couch to clasp the woman in his arms, at the same time tugging the ring from her finger. She woke with a gasp, flinched, and struggled to push him away.

'Get... off... me!' she hissed between startled breaths. But as she twisted in his arms, he found unfamiliar stirrings surging through his body, and a stiffening between his legs. For these sensations he had no name.

'I'm terribly *hungry*!' he exclaimed in an attempt to give them one.

'Well **I** won't be your meal!' Jeschute spat, and then saw a way to distract him, 'There's food over there on the table!'

Indeed, bread and roast fowl lay where she pointed, and these the youth, trying to still the strange currents coursing through his veins, fell upon ravenously. As she watched him, Jeschute could see that he was more simple-minded than vicious.

'My husband will be back at any moment, and if he sees you here he'll be furious!' she said, hoping to scare him away.

'If you don't want to see him upset, I'll leave,' replied the other generously, and stepped out through the tent flap.

'Leave my ring!' she yelled, but the puzzling answer came back,

'My mother told me I must keep it!' and he was gone.

Hardly a moment had passed before Orilus came riding back into the clearing. He was a large, forceful man who had spent his whole life in command. He saw, quite clearly, tracks in the dew-soaked grass, leading to his wife's tent and then away from it again.

Entering the tent, he found his wife flushed and dishevelled.

'Your lover and I...' he fumed, 'have only just failed to meet. But meet we shall!'

'No...!' she wailed, and then let fall from her lips the disastrous words, '...it was just a youth I'd never seen before.' Raging, Orilus began to stride to and fro. Seizing the bedcover, he tore it nearly in two. Grasping his wife's saddle, he smashed it down, and then again, and again so that it began to come apart.

'This is what you'll wear in future', he bellowed, holding up the tattered bedding, 'and this,' gesturing at the broken saddle, 'is what you'll ride on!' Thus he meant to parade his wife, disgraced and scorned before the eyes of all the world.

The youth, meanwhile, heard a piercing shriek which echoed among the leaves. And coming to a clearing, he saw a young woman cradling in her lap the head of a knight who lay before her in the stillness of death.

'God help you!' he offered, then explaining. 'My mother told me to greet everyone politely.' Then his manner switched.

'Tell me who has done this thing!' he demanded, 'and I'll go after him and do the same to him.' The young woman, Sigune, looked up, touched that one so green should be so ready to help.

'What is your name?' she asked, wonderingly.

'Beloved Son, I was sometimes called...,' he replied, '...or else Dear Son, or Beautiful Son...' At these words she began to gaze at him intently.

'I think I know who you are...' she said, now thoughtful, 'your mother is my aunt, Herzeloyde. This man died defending lands that by right of birth are yours. He had declared his love for me, and how bitterly I now regret that I delayed in returning it.'

'Then tell me who has done this to him!' the young man persisted, 'so that I can go after him.'

'I can see', said Sigune, 'that you have the ability to go straight to the centre of any matter you come upon, so I declare your name from now on should be **Parsifal**, which means 'straight through the middle'. I once heard your mother say that was what she intended.'

'Yes, if you think that's a good one', came the other, 'but now tell me where whoever did this has gone, so I can chase after him'.

'He took that path', she answered, pointing with careful deliberation in exactly the opposite direction to the one the attacker had taken, for she was quite certain that otherwise harm would befall one who seemed so unknowing.

★ ★ ★ ★ ★

Soon he came to a wide sweep of meadow, wildflowers of many colours intermingled with its long grasses. Beyond it stood the walls of a city, and cantering towards him from that direction, a knight, red from the tip of his lance to the last hair of his great horse's tail.

He pulled up before Parsifal. His face was fine-featured but dauntless, with an edge of resentment.

'Would you do me a service' he asked, 'if you are going into that city?'

'God help you!' replied the other, 'my mother told me to greet everyone politely. Yes, I'll do the service. I'm going to Arthur to ask him to make me a knight.'
The horseman suppressed a smile. 'Then take a message from me, Ither, to Arthur, who presides there. Tell him that I lay claim to the throne of Britain, and will contest for it against any champion he sends to face me.'

'I think I can remember that,' said the young man, concentrating hard, willing to help, but far from used to the terms he was hearing.

When he came through the city gate, his sacking suit, javelin, ancient pony and wide eyes immediately attracted a great crowd of gawpers. 'God help you all!' he blurted at them. 'My mother told me to greet everyone politely. Which way to Arthur?' The gawpers gleefully gestured him on and trailed after him as he made his way through the streets. Soon he passed into the Great Hall and saw the dazzling throng of men and women, sumptuously clothed, who mingled there. They filled the room in knots and clusters, milling around a mass of tables, with one set apart at the far end. Among them stood the graceful form of the Lady Cunneware, who never laughed. A sorcerer had once foretold of her that it would remain so until she laid eyes on the man who would gain the highest of all honours. Also there was the dumb jester Antenor, of whom the same man had said that he would never speak until Cunneware laughed.

'Whichever one of you is Arthur,' called out Parsifal, looking around him at all the magnificence, 'God help you! I bring a message from... him, outside the gates. He... wants to fight someone, and I want to have clothes and gear just like his!' There were sniggers and titters all round the hall. Arthur, however, eyed him shrewdly from the high table.

'It may just be,' he said, as all hushed to listen, 'that you have the makings of a knight. But that would only be decided after careful consideration, and certainly not before tomorrow.'

'But if I fought him really well, then couldn't I have his stuff!' insisted Parsifal, and again there was a wave of sniggering.

'That would be much too dangerous for you, my young cocksparrow!' Arthur replied, not unkindly. But the knight Keie, the King's ill-tempered Steward, had been watching all this and was much irritated by the way in which this half-wit seemed to earn so much attention. Now he saw a way to make him come to grief.

'My King', he urged, 'surely you would not have it said that Arthur refused a heartfelt entreaty it was in his power to grant?.'

'That's right!' chimed in the young newcomer, understanding only that Keie was urging the King to agree to his request. Arthur looked from one to the other, saw one face full of unaccustomed encouragement, the other of enormous eagerness. Whatever his misgivings, he felt propelled by some secret momentum in these events, and with a resigned nod he gave his assent.

There was a general cry of excitement and many surged forward as Parsifal remounted, to follow him out and see what would happen. But as he moved towards the doorway on his bedraggled old pony, dressed in his sacking suit, his chin puckered in determination, a peal of laughter cascaded through the air. And those nearby turned in astonishment, for it had come from the throat of Cunneware, the lady who never laughed.

'You've refused to honour any of us with your laughter' thundered Keie, the steward, as he lurched in fury towards her, 'and now you laugh at this numbskull!' He grasped her hair, he wrapped it round his wrist, he raised his staff and he struck her on the back.

'Though she is beaten now because of him,' came a voice, 'one day, Keie, the same will happen to you!' And those close by gasped, startled once more, for these words had fallen from the lips of Antenor, the dumb jester. But Keie, his fury redoubled, ran at Antenor with his staff raised to strike again. Parsifal, pressed towards the doorway by the excited crowd, looked back and saw all this take place. Knowing that he was somehow the cause, he instantly felt compelled to find some way of making amends.

When Parsifal's pony plodded up to the spot where Ither waited, and its rider said
'None of them wanted to fight you, so they sent me!' the knight went slack-jawed in disbelief.

'They've sent you?' he echoed, doubting his own ears. But as he sat there all hesitation, Parsifal took advantage by grasping a strap upon his armour and tugging it hard as if hoping it would come away and into his possession. The other, in sudden and angry reflex, lashed out at pony and rider with the full length of his lance-shaft, and they tumbled sprawling upon the grass.

Filled with rage, the youth scrambled to his feet, grasping his javelin. Then he hurled it. He had grown up running free in the forest, strong of arm and keen of eye. And the javelin point passed straight through the slit between Ither's helmet and its visor. Ither crashed to the ground, his brains pierced, lifeless. Scarcely knowing what he was doing, Parsifal then began to fumble with the straps and buckles of Ither's armour.

'What a one you are!' came a voice. A young squire had run out from the city, excited and astounded, and now proceeded to help the other put on Ither's armour. For the moment, Parsifal's dazed excitement was such that he gave the corpse no further thought.

'What a story this'll make!' chattered the squire, as he worked. Eventually Parsifal stood, clad from head to foot in red armour, and before him the great war horse. But he had only sat upon bare-backed forest ponies, and a stirrup meant nothing to him. So, as if at home and not weighed down by a casing of metal, he took a run and a huge leap and landed with a clatter in the saddle. The watching squire, unlike Parsifal himself, knew what an extraordinary feat this was and gasped. The latter now touched the horse's flank gingerly with the long spurs he was wearing for the first time, and instantly it lunged forward into a headlong gallop. Over humps and bumps it leapt, through the branches of the trees they crashed. Nor did Parsifal have any idea how to stop his horse, and so it galloped on, through thickets and glades and across hillsides and streams, swerving corners, stretching into long strides where the going was straight and flat. The sun had crossed the sky and the horse sped on, until even Parsifal's strong body cried out for an end to the jolting and rocking.

Only as evening approached did the red horse slow down to a walk of its own accord just as they neared a sturdy castle casting long shadows on the cleared ground around it. Just outside its gate a man stood, grey-haired but vigorous, with his falcon upon his wrist.

'My mother told me,' blurted out Parsifal instantly between panting breaths, 'that a man grey in the years of his head would be wise and be able to teach me... will you? Can you tell me what knights do? How do I make this horse stop when I want it to? How do I take this clothing off for the night? My mother told me to keep any ring a woman let me have, but I don't know what to do with it, will you tell me?'

The other eyed the newcomer with puzzled interest. Then he spoke,
'Your manners and your horsemanship are appalling. But I can see that your heart is open. Come in and be welcome.' This was Gurnemanz, well known as a tutor of young men in the ways of knighthood. He led Parsifal to the courtyard, where they were met by a fresh-faced girl of about sixteen, followed by three others.
'This is my daughter Liaze,' said Gurnemanz, and to her 'I entrust him to you, my dear. Make him comfortable for the night.'

So they led him to a bedchamber where Liaze and one of her friends began to unbuckle and remove the metal plates, while the others poured buckets of steaming water into a bath. They found his figure admirably well formed, but his manner odd. For when he had clambered awkwardly into the bath, when they massaged and lathered his bruised body, exclaiming,
'What fine shoulders you have!' and other enthusiastic comments, he became ever more shy and confused. When at last they waited for him to arise, he remained

sitting resolutely upright in the water. Until, finally, he blurted nervously,
'I must have a robe!' So, stifling their mischievous laughter, they handed one over, and left him to himself.

The next morning, Gurnemanz began to teach Parsifal the knightly codes of conduct.

'You must,' he instructed 'stop talking about your mother all the time, you are now an adult. Also, it is most unseemly to shower people with questions as soon as you come to a new place. This must definitely stop, otherwise people will think you are a half-wit'. Much else Gurnemanz explained. At one point he said,
'A knight may seek fame and the rapture of victory. He may feel thrilled by the magnificence of his armour, his gear and his horse. But in the end, he must know that victory or defeat are granted to him by the Grace of God. That his task is the steadfast defence of those under his protection, whether they be women, children, holy men, a blessed King or sacred land. All I can tell you about women,' he concluded, 'is this. Man and woman are bound together as closely as the sun and the day itself. They grow from one stem'.

So he led his pupil out to the turf where several young men were already at practice with horse and lance. First Gurnemanz spent time on the finer points of horsemanship – such as how to stop. When Parsifal seemed to have some grasp of these, he handed a lance up to him. Then he called to another of the young men.

'Ride against him. Let's see how he does!' So the two, on champing horses, drew off to face each other. They put lance to rest and their mounts leapt forward. The ground shook as they thundered at each other and met with a crash and a thud as a body hit the ground. The one who remained in his saddle was Parsifal.

The brow of Gurnemanz furrowed in muted surprise. 'You!' he uttered, turning to another of his pupils, 'try against him also.' So Parsifal faced his second opponent. Again they waited for the sign, thundered forward, clashed, and again it was Parsifal who remained mounted. Then this happened with a third, fourth and fifth opponent. Gurnemanz turned away, pondering deeply.

That evening his whispered to his daughter, Liaze, 'Do sit with him if you wish. Cut up his meat like an attentive hostess. It will do no harm if your hands touch.'

She was far from unwilling to do as her father urged, for the young man's good looks were exceptional. Parsifal gave no sign that the young woman's attention were unwelcome. Though novel to him, he began to find them very pleasant.

For many strenuous months the training continued and Parsifal meanwhile gained a little more fluency in the language of the wide world. Then came the evening that Gurnemanz called his pupil over to the fireside and said, 'Young man, never have I seen anyone with greater natural aptitude for battle and the joust than you.' His glance moved back and forth between the flames and his listener's face. 'Three sons I have lost on the field of war. You already know my daughter... I urge you to stay, marry her and become the heir to all that is mine...'

'My teacher,' Parsifal replied, 'I know this is the greatest honour you could offer anyone. But I cannot accept it. How can I know my true worth as a knight until I have faced real enemies out in the world. How can I know I deserve a woman's hand? For the time being at least, I must refuse the honour you offer me.'

Gurnemanz recognised the determination in the other's eye. 'With those words,' he said gravely, 'I lose a fourth son. But so it must be'. Soon after, with sad faces watching his dwindling figure, Parsifal rode out through the gates of Gurnemanz' castle and towards the trees.

★ ★ ★ ★ ★

For many hours Parsifal let his horse pick the path. In this way he reached the further edge of the forest and looked out on a great walled city set beside the sparkling sea. Before it, there rose a vast hum of gruff voices, and the sound of mallets on wood and hammers on metal. An army was encamped and waiting to overrun the city. The smoke of their numberless cookfires twisted skywards.

The warring forces had wearily left off fighting just before Parsifal arrived, and he rode unhindered towards a gate. It was opened from within by watchful men-at-arms who seemed to assume he had come to join them and stood back to let him pass.

As he rode along the streets of that city, he saw on all sides sad eyes, hungry faces, broken weapons and dented armour.
'Come this way, Sir,' beckoned one man carrying a spear, while another grasped his rein. He was led up stairways and through halls until he stood before the young queen of that city. And at that moment, something very new awakened inside him. It went far

beyond the strange hunger Jeschute had aroused in him as he lay beside her in her tent. The sight of this other stirred his heart to its very roots. In spite of this, he well remembered the rules his teacher Gurnemanz had laid down. He didn't just refrain from asking questions. He uttered not a word.

'He can't like the sight of me very much', thought Condwiramurs, the Queen, 'maybe our lack of food is affecting my looks. Or could it be,' she then thought, noticing his hesitant manner, 'that he thinks it impolite to speak before his hostess? Tell me, sir,' she asked, 'where you have travelled from?'

So he told her of Gurnemanz.

'He is my dear uncle,' she forced a smile, 'and how I wish he was here now. But perhaps your coming is just as fortunate as if he'd come himself.' Then she shared with him the meagre meal of a few scraps which was all that could be found. Next he was conducted to a bed chamber in which he soon sank into a sound sleep.

But in the depths of the night, his door opened cautiously and through it crept Condwiramurs in her nightgown of white silk. She had found her command over her own actions suddenly weak. Nearly sick with the worry of ruling a town besieged by a strong enemy, she longed for company and comfort. And she felt herself irresistibly drawn to this strange young man. Torn by her own impulses, she sank to her knees beside his bed and began to sob with vexation.

He stirred, blinked, then opened his eyes very wide and sat bolt upright.

'If I got out of bed,' he dithered, 'maybe you can get under the covers and then you won't have to kneel there shivering on the floor...'

'We could both be warm under the same covers...' she whispered, 'as long as you can show... restraint'. The implications lost on him, quite unaware of her full meaning, Parsifal mumbled in bewilderment and made room. Then he found their bodies alongside each other and it felt glorious, but very strange. So they lay there in hesitant fondness and she told him her story.

'My father was King of this city of Belrepeire. When he died – only months ago – I became Queen. But then the King Clamide laid claim to both the city and myself. I'm at my wit's end. Over half the men have died defending the walls. But I'd rather throw myself from those walls than deliver myself to him.'

'Tomorrow,' responded Parsifal with wrinkled brow, 'I'll do whatever I can...' And they fell asleep side by side.

In the bright morning, as Clamide's entire army stood arrayed before the city on the point of assault, Parsifal rode out through the gates alone.

The attackers were enthralled by such rashness.

'Now what on earth does he think he's doing?' muttered an archer, shaking his head. No fighter lifted a finger to stop him as he passed through rank upon rank of Clamide's men. Close he came to the spot where the King himself sat on his charger.

'She sends a champion!' commented Clamide to his companions, 'It seems fitting that I should meet him alone.'

So now he trotted down from his hillock until they both reached an area of level ground. There they squared off, facing each other, and couched their lances. Then came the leap forwards and the pounding of hooves. They met each other headlong, each striking the other's body armour yet gripping to their saddles. Both horses reared up with the effort, then both girths snapped and both riders tumbled. As they scrambled to their feet sword in hand, Clamide felt the weight of boulders hurled from a great height falling upon his armoured body.

'You have helpers on the walls throwing rocks at me!' he yelled at his opponent, 'this is against all rules of single combat!'

'I assure you,' panted Parsifal from under his helm, 'that the only blows falling upon you are those of my sword!' and so it was. Clamide now knew he had never faced such might. He was hammered to the ground and felt his helm ripped from his head and saw the other's sword hanging above his throat.

'I offer you your life,' said Parsifal gravely, 'but only if you give up all claim to this city and its Queen, and you present yourself to the court of Arthur and pledge service there to a lady who was beaten because of me.'

Clamide gasped for breath, then screwed up his face, then spoke: 'I will do these things.'

Within an hour, the people of Condwiramurs's city watched from their ramparts as the army of Clamide dismantled its camp and began to march away. That night, Parsifal and Condwiramurs lay under the coverlets together again. This time the embraces were keen and full of sighs. So new to the arts of love were both, though, that those embraces remained uncompleted.

But a second and a third night followed, and during these they learned their sweet lessons well.

Their marriage soon after began a golden time, in which each wanted nothing more than the company of the other. They enjoyed, in addition, the gratitude and regard of the townsfolk, and all this, as the weeks flowed by, seemed unceasing.

So it was with a heart well full that Parsifal said one evening,

'I think it is time, beloved, that I went to see how my mother fares.'

'Then make your absence as brief as you can,' came the reply, 'for I shall regret every moment of it.' Soon after, he rode out through the gates of Belrepeire, the city of Condwiramurs, uncertain of his route.

II: Outcast

Now the knight came to a region of dank pools, rotting undergrowth and broken trees, In the midst of it lay a lake on which he could see boats. The men and women in them were richly clothed and one wore a many-hued hat made all of peacock feathers. But the face beneath it was haggard, as if marked by some long anguish. Nevertheless, as Parsifal rode along the edge of the lake, this man gestured in greeting.

'My castle,' he called, 'lies further on. Be welcome there and I'll join you this evening.'

When Parsifal reached the castle he found it had the sturdiest and most cunningly crafted walls and gates he had ever seen, but it was strangely hushed. There was no sound of voices, labour or music. When he came across the drawbridge and onto the jousting ground, he found the turf unmarked by hooves. Kindly young men appeared though, took his horse and conducted him to superbly furnished rooms where they helped him disarm and gave him a cloak made from cloth of gold to cover his travel-worn garments.
'It is lent by Repanse de Schoye,' one of them confided, 'whom you will see later and surely never forget the sight of her!'

They led him to a great banqueting hall, filled with men and women sumptuously dressed. And as he looked about him wide-eyed, Parsifal knew that he had never seen such tapestries as hung there, for every human activity seemed lavishly pictured upon them. Nor such curtains and cushions, for every fruit and leaf in the world seemed to be portrayed in the fabrics, every colour displayed. The many fires in that hall burned only the most smokeless and aromatic of logs. At the far end of the hall the host was propped on a couch, but now swaddled in thick furs as if the room was in fact deathly cold. Next to him waited an empty place for the guest.

Hardly had he sat down, when a dark chant began to arise from the throats of everyone in the room. As it grew louder, it became a doleful moan, rising to its sharpest as the door at one end of the room opened, and in came a youth carrying aloft a great spear. Blood flowed from the lance tip, down the shaft and onto the hand and sleeve of the bearer. He carried it along the four walls of the hall, reaching each of the four corners, before leaving the way he had come, as the moaning at last faded away.

Then two young women entered in shimmering gowns of brown silk with flowers woven into their hair, carrying golden candelabra. Two more followed carrying trestle stands made of ivory. Then four whose gowns were green, bearing more candles, followed by another four, each holding the corner of a table top crafted entirely from a single red-hued garnet. This priceless table was set upon its ivory stands before Parsifal's host. Two other dazzling young women now entered, their gowns shot with gold, their hands clasping silver carving knives. Four more came, dressed likewise, with more candelabra, and then six with crystal lamps in which soothing balsam smouldered.

Then it was as if the sun rose at the far end of the room. For a maiden had entered carrying, on a cushion, a great gemstone. It shone and glimmered such that it was impossible to make out its exact shape. This gemstone she placed upon a stool in the centre of the room. Then came serving men with bowls, plates and jugs. Each one tilted his vessel towards the gemstone and in that instant it became filled to the brim with food or drink. Meats, breads, fruits, wines, and more, each of the rarest and most delicious. And these were then carried to every corner of the room and offered to those seated.

As he watched all these things, Parsifal was as filled with puzzlement as those bowls were with food. But he well remembered the instructions of Gurnemanz,
'It is most unseemly to shower people with questions as soon as you come to a new place...' and so he said nothing. When the feast had continued for some time, a servant stepped forward carrying a gleaming sword. The scabbard was the purest gold, the hilt the reddest ruby.

'This sword,' said Parsifal's host, 'never failed me in battle. But such exploits are beyond me now. Receive my sword as my gift, that it may guard your life.'
'My heartfelt thanks, Sir,' was all the dazed Parsifal could say.

When the meal was finished, the procession once again took place, though this time, in reverse order with the gemstone first, and the groups of young women following. Soon after, the host turned gravely to Parsifal with the words,
'If you are weary from your travel, your bed awaits you.'
So Parsifal withdrew from the room utterly silent and soon slept, not knowing that this was the Grail Castle, his host was the Grail King, and the last maiden in the procession, Repanse de Schoye, had carried the Grail itself. The night though, was marked by dreams in which that happened which never did in waking life: Parsifal's flesh was hacked by swords and skewered by lance points.

When he awoke next morning he knew instantly that the place was even more hushed than when he first arrived.

No one came to attend him and awkwardly he donned his armour alone. He stepped out of his bedchamber into an empty corridor. He passed from room to room, but found no sign of any person, nor the slightest murmur of a voice. Alarm began to grip his heart as he hurried along the corridors. But still he found not a single soul.

He did find his horse, in the courtyard, well-fed and glossily groomed but saddled and standing at the mounting block ready for departure. Seeing no better course of action, he swung into the saddle and rode through the gate. The instant he had passed through, the portcullis fell with a clang that shook the ground.

'May the sun pour down hatred upon you instead of warmth!' came a bitter cry from the battlements. 'You who could have spoken the question which would have brought an end to all our sorrow, but did not!' and Parsifal saw one young man, high on the battlements, jabbing a finger at him viciously. Appalled, but understanding nothing of this, Parsifal turned away. Now he saw trampled grass which marked the passage of a great company of riders, who must have left the castle before he arose.

As, perplexed, he once more passed under the boughs of the forest, a spine-chilling wail tore the air. He came before a linden tree, and saw pain-filled eyes looking down at him from its branches. A young woman was seated up there, and draped across the boughs in front of her, an armoured corpse. Her head was almost entirely without hair, as if she had pulled it out in handfuls. But as Parsifal approached, he recognised Sigune, who had given him his name the day after he left his mother, and who still grieved ceaselessly over her slain beloved.

'It's you,' she mouthed wonderingly, 'whom I named Parsifal. Have you come from the Castle at Munsalvaesche?' He nodded.

'I see', she continued, 'that you carry the sword of Anfortas himself. The sword that will shatter. But then if placed under the waters of the spring at Karnant before dawn, the pieces will join again and be stronger than any other. Did you know this?' He shook his head. 'Did you', she went on eagerly, 'ask the question they all waited to hear?' If you did, not only will the Fisher King be healed, but you will know good fortune beyond all bounds!' Parsifal met her eyes, grim-faced.

'I asked no question.' he replied. Instantly her face became a grimace of fury, her eyes as if filled with venom. 'You saw how much that man suffered,' she yelled, 'but you did not bother to ask what caused it? How I wish you were far from this spot, so that my eyes did not have to look upon you.' Parsifal recoiled as if he had been struck on the cheek, then turned away shamefaced and confused. Without another word he rode off.

Soon, following a track, he found himself catching up with another rider. But her bedraggled horse limped, her saddle seemed to be held together by scraps of old rope and she was clad in a torn bedcover. As he came alongside her, she turned her careworn face to look at him.

'It's you!' she spat instantly, 'You who caused all my misery!'

'I've never harmed any woman!' he blurted, perplexed, only then beginning to recognise Jeschute, the wife of Orilus the Duke whom he had disturbed in her tent so many months before. And only now did he become aware of Orilus himself who rode far ahead, intending thus to exhibit his wife's shame.

But the Duke, hearing voices, turned and saw his wife conversing with an armoured knight. As was the custom, therefore, he wheeled his horse and made ready to joust. His shield and his helmet both bore the device of a dragon with great flaring wings. The two knights thundered at each other and met with a splintering of wood as both lances shattered. Then the swords were out and the sun flashed upon the whirling blades. Long they fought, until Orilus leaned close and seized hold of Parsifal with both arms seeking to pull him from the saddle. The other reacted instantly by clasping his arms around Orilus and heaving as he braced in the stirrups. They crashed to the ground together but with Parsifal on top, blood streaming from Orilus's nose and Parsifal's sword held poised in the air above Orilus's chest.

'I'd be pleased to grant your life,' said the younger, 'but only if you promise to restore this lady to her former place as one honoured and cherished.'

The battered Orilus hesitated briefly, then breathed 'I agree to it.'

'Come with me then to some holy place where I can make a solemn oath,' continued Parsifal, 'for it was I who came to your tent that day and with my oath I can put your heart at ease.'

'The cave of the hermit Trevrizent is nearby,' answered Orilus, beginning to understand the other's intentions. So they all rode towards a place where the forest was broken up by crags and cliff-faces.

As they arrived at the cave, the aged Trevrizent, gaunt and coarse-robed, but with eyes full of sympathy, came out to meet them.

'I wish to make a solemn oath' Parsifal confided to him.

'I have a casket containing the bones of a saint, over which I am accustomed to pray,' offered Trevrizent, 'you could place your hand upon it.'

So Parsifal stood before them all by Trevrizent's hallowed casket.

'I swear,' he said, 'that the lady Jeschute showed me no favour when I came upon her in her tent that day, an unknowing fool in a world which was strange to me. Indeed, I had to struggle with her to pull the ring from her finger. Here,' and he held it up before them, 'I now return it to her.'

'What anguish you have ended with those words!' sighed Orilus, as he took his cloak and placed it tenderly around his wife's shoulders. 'All this time I have longed for us to be united again. But I could not bear the thought that she might prefer another!'

'Stay, tell us your story!' begged Jeschute through happy tears, 'let us see if we can outdo whatever hospitality you have ever received!' But he refused all their entreaties. Instead, stricken by his memories of the Grail Castle, he set off to roam the forests and battlefields of the world. In the years that followed, he threw himself into as many contests as he could find, and in all he remained undefeated. This, however, did nothing to soothe his loathing of his own self.

★ ★ ★ ★ ★

Beneath the blossoming boughs, a camp of many tents and pavilions spreads throughout the forest. It is Maytime, but in the night snow has fallen and now covers the ground. Arthur and all his retinue have travelled here in search of the Red Knight, for so many warriors defeated by him have arrived at the court with pledges of service and news of his exploits. The King intends to offer him a place in the fellowship of the Round Table.

A young squire has wandered away from the main camp and into a forest clearing, where he spies a stranger knight, sitting on his horse motionless and staring at the ground. The armour of this stranger knight is thoroughly stained with rust and mud so that you cannot see exactly what colour it's supposed to be. Likewise the caparison of his horse.

The squire runs back to the camp, sees the knight Segramors, and tells him what he's seen. Segramors is a young warrior, but swift and fierce.
'A stranger near the camp! It's my privilege, then,' he announces, 'to challenge him to joust. Help me arm!'

Soon after, Segramors rides out to the clearing. His saddle creaks satisfyingly, his limbs feel supple and well rested. He sees the stranger just as the squire has left him, staring fixedly at the very same spot of snow-covered earth. Segramors rides to a place where he turns and makes ready to charge. It is the other's horse, though not its rider, who cocks its ears, who lifts its head in response, who turns to face the challenger. The rider attends only to the snow. The horse springs forward as soon as Segramors' mount starts its onrush. It is only now, hurtling at full pelt, that the stranger seems to rouse from his stupor. But when they crash together with a jarring of metal and wood, it is Segramors who tumbles to the ground.

For the stranger is Parsifal. He had ridden that way upon the twists and turns of his wandering. He had arrived at a spot where a goose caught by a falcon had left three drops of blood in the snow. The moment he had cast eyes on that red tinge on the white, the memory of Condwiramurs, of her cheeks and lips, had arisen before him. And this exquisite dream-picture had wiped out everything else. He had been held fast by it. His red horse, well-accustomed to the business of jousting, had needed no guidance from its rider when it heard galloping hooves approaching.

Such was the lure of the dream-picture, though, that as soon as his horse slowed from its charge, Parsifal wheeled it straight back to the very same place, and stared once more at that spot where the vision of his lost wife had become so real.

When the battered Segramors limped back into camp, and when Keie, Arthur's ill-tempered steward, saw him, the latter barked,
'It's my privilege, then, to avenge this insult to the fellowship of the Round Table!' Soon he was armed and mounted and trotted out to the clearing. The stranger had not moved. Keie rode up close enough for them to touch.

'You might as well,' he sneered, 'buckle a collar around your neck and give the other end of the leash to me, so I can lead you back into the camp!' But the other did not even look up. Furious, Keie now struck the stranger's shield with the shaft of his lance. Still the other did not stir.

Snorting his disgust, Keie withdrew to prepare his charge, wheeled and lurched toward his opponent. Again it was Parsifal's horse which showed some understanding of his rider's predicament, perked up and shot forward towards the attacker. Again, it was only now with his eyes wrenched from the snow, that Parsifal awoke from his trance and lowered his lance. But as they collided, he sent the opposing horse and rider reeling backwards over a fallen tree trunk and onto the jagged rocks behind it. The horse was killed outright. The rider lay writhing with an arm and one leg broken. But Parsifal barely noticed, turning away again to that red tinge in the snow, and the image of Condwiramurs.

When Keie was carried back moaning into the camp, Gawain, the King's nephew, watched thoughtfully. He had been nurtured from his earliest days in the codes of knighthood. He'd had the best tutors and followed their path with devotion. He decided a more cautious and peaceable approach than Keie's was called for here. Unarmed he rode out to the glade, and walked his horse up to the newcomer, who still sat staring at the ground.

Gawain followed the direction of the other's eyes, and saw the blood upon the snow. Unwinding his scarf from around his neck, he leaned forward in his saddle and dropped it, so that it landed straight on the redness. Now the other blinked and looked up like one awakened.

'Would you come back to the camp with me,' asked Gawain kindly, 'and meet the King?'

'What camp?' came the other's dazed voice, 'who are you?'

'Gawain, I am called,' came the smiling answer, 'and pleased I'd be to call you friend. The camp is that of Arthur, and you, I believe, are the one we have come to find.'

'Then I cannot come,' Parsifal responded gravely, 'for I made a vow never to visit the Court of Arthur again until I had avenged the lady who was beaten because of me the day I first came there.'

'Then put your mind at ease,' laughed Gawain, 'for that you have just done. It was Keie who struck her, and Cunneware herself is waiting at the tents to congratulate you on your victory!'

When, soon after, Parsifal sat in place of honour beside Arthur, at the Round Table that had been pitched out in the open, when he'd been kissed and sighed over by Cunneware, when he had been welcomed with cries of good fellowship by that whole company, then for the first time in a very long while, well-being began to creep towards him. He answered Gawain's smiles with his own, he readily let his hand rest in the slender hand of Cunneware.

From the forest depths came the thud of approaching hooves. As everyone looked up, a rider on a large mule came into view and rode towards the table. They could see it was a woman from her gown, but her face was covered by a dark gauzy veil. Her hands, though, were like the talons of some swooping hawk. When she halted and lifted the cloth from her face, there were gasps of dread around the glade. She had teeth like the tusks of a wild boar. Her ears were like those of a bear, her eyebrows so thick and long that they had been braided, and her eyes flickered with fierceness. Yet many there knew that this woman was fluent in many languages, and skilled in every art, for it was Cundrie, the Sorceress.

'No longer,' she called, 'does the Round Table mean excellence. For Parsifal sits at it, he who could have mouthed the question which would have ended the pain of the Grail King, but failed to do so! He, who would then have received such wealth that he would have been even richer than his brother, the man both black and white, who rules six lands far across the seas!'

A great sob now arose from deep within her breast. Then another came, then more, and sobbing she turned to ride away.

But as she did so, the pounding of other hooves was heard, and from a different direction a horseman came into the clearing, bespattered with mud from a long, fast journey.

'There is a blemish on the great name of the Round Table!' he yelled, as if echoing the words of Cundrie, but then went on, 'and that is Gawain, who slew the father of my King, Vergulaht, in the very moment of receiving his greeting as host. I therefore challenge him to meet me in single combat at the place called Schampfanzun as soon as he can reach there!' Swinging his horse around, he swept out of sight.

Both new-found friends were stunned as by a lance thrust. Parsifal's wound was re-opened by Cundrie's words and he was mystified by news of a brother. Gawain was stung by an accusation he did not understand. But each now prepared to leave.

'May God watch over you, my friend,' said Gawain.

'And return you safely to us,' echoed Cunneware.

'God,' answered the crestfallen Parsifal, 'cares nothing for me.' Soon, helped by Cunneware's fond hands, he mounted up and trotted away, sad-eyed. Gawain took a different path.

III: Lover

As Gawain rode, every inch of him, and his gear and his famed horse Gringolet, spoke of his breeding and training. That he was the nephew of Arthur himself was evident in his bearing. He had only been a few days out when, emerging from the trees, he viewed a column of knights trudging doggedly along the road. Many more spears, many hooves and marching feet followed, their sound like the ceaseless surging of the sea, upon a shingle beach.

Gawain urged his horse forward and raised his hand to halt a rider at the tail end of a column.

'What army is this?' he asked.
'These,' the other answered as his mount fidgeted, 'are the men of King Meljanz, or of his friends and relations. They go to attack the fortress of Duke Lyppaut. Meljanz, you see, grew up in the household of Lyppaut. Then he fell head over heels for one of the Duke's daughters. But she told him she preferred to remain free to receive proposals from greater kings, if she fancied. He was furious, and claimed that her father had turned her against him. Then he stormed off to raise this army and attack Lyppaut.'

When, soon after, Gawain came before the sprawling fortress, he saw its walls packed with defenders, but the slopes all around swarmed with even more attackers. Curious, but hesitant, he made his way towards a clump of trees near the gates. As he arrived there, he noticed three female figures watching from the walls above.

'Now who could that be?' he heard the eldest ask.

'I guess, from the look of him, a horse-trader or a shield-salesman perhaps!' the middle one replied with determined scorn.

'You're so mean!' scolded the youngest, still well under twelve years old, 'he's so fine-looking he must be really brave, and I'd ever so much like him to offer me his service!'

The first of these was the mother of the other two. They were Obie, who had managed to spark the disappointed fury of Meljanz the young King, and Obilot her little sister. When Meljanz had lived in their household, Obie had found that whenever he was near it set her all quivering. She had decided, therefore – as is often the way – that she couldn't bear him, and had spoken words to send him packing. So now she couldn't bear any other young men, because they were not him, nor would she hear any suggestion that they might be his equal. Such are the knots in which the heart can tie itself.

'Open the gate enough to let that man in,' ordered Lyppaut, who watched from a different vantage point. Then he waited to greet Gawain within the walls. His beard was grey, his eyes careworn, but appreciative.

'It's good,' he said warmly, 'to see such a well-equipped knight joining us.'

'I fear I must disappoint you,' answered Gawain, his own regret clear in his eyes, 'my good name depends on my meeting a challenger soon in Vergulaht's city, so I cannot stay...'

The moment he paused, scurrying feet announced the arrival of Obilot.

'If you'll be my knight and fight for me,' she blurted in a gust of eagerness, 'then I'll grant you all of my love straight away!'

Every code that Gawain followed compelled him to accept such an offer, but voiced privately and with much more discretion by a grown woman and not a small girl. Now he faced a dilemma. Should he risk disappointing the child, or risk the mockery of other adults for accepting her scheme? For it would mean riding out before all eyes bearing on his war-gear the love-token of a child.

'I am honoured,' he replied firmly, audible to all around, 'to accept your gracious offer.'

'Mother, mother, I must have a token to give my knight!' shrilled the girl, scampering off through the bystanders.

As the early mists of the following morning began to rise, they revealed the countless ranks of Meljanz advancing. Three sets of gates creaked open and through each a column of Lyppaut's men surged outwards. Near the head of one, galloped Gawain, a silken sleeve fastened upon his shield. His first foe had the slope against him and came down before Gawain. Fired by the thrill of this early victory, he then carved a path across the battlefield, leaving riderless horses and wounded men behind him. His companions took heart, redoubled their own efforts and for the first time during that siege the tide turned against Meljanz.

Close by the gates, each turning away from their latest foe, Gawain and the young King, Meljanz came face to face. They spurred their horses at each other and Meljanz found himself hurled to the ground by Gawain's lance. As he struggled to rise and draw his sword he felt a searing pain in the arm, for the lance had pierced it. As the strength drained from Meljanz's body, Gawain seized him under the armpit and tugged him forcefully towards the gate, which watchers now opened just enough to let them through.

'If only,' winced the badly weakened Meljanz, 'you had met the Red Knight who fights on my side! Then you could not have won this day for Lyppaut!' But Gawain inwardly gave all thanks that he had not been forced to cross swords with his friend, Parsifal.

Now he lifted from his shield the silken sleeve Obilot had given him as a token. It scarcely held together, having been slashed by many blades and splashed with blood and mud. He sent a servant with it to the women's quarters where the delighted Obilot waved it in her sister's face.

'Whose knight brought this back from the fight?' she smirked.

The banqueting hall was crowded that evening with Lyppaut's men and the many opponents who had been compelled to surrender earlier. When Obilot hurried in, Gawain followed strictly the rules of his calling,

'These men,' he said to her, 'I leave at your command, especially as I must soon go to complete the task awaiting me elsewhere.'

'There is none,' responded Meljanz himself, showing all the charm and grace which his hurt fury with Obie had swept away. 'I would be happier to obey.'

'Well,' trilled Obilot imperiously, 'I command you instead to offer obedience to my sister, and,' she was beginning to discover a flare for giving orders, 'I command my sister to accept it.'

Meljanz and Obie peered resentfully and hesitantly at each other, and then the ferocity drained from the face of each at the same moment. From beneath the folds of Obie's robe her hand peeped and then slid up the man's injured arm as her lips brushed the place where he was wounded. The few halting words which then passed between them quickly became a torrent of ardent conversation, which was clearly for the ears of nobody else.

'I much regret,' Gawain now explained to the grateful Lyppaut and his wife, 'that I must leave at first light.'

'No you mustn't! No you won't! No you can't,' yelled Obilot tearfully, and it was only when her mother firmly unclasped the girl's hands from Gawain's clothing that he was able to go and seek his rest.

★ ★ ★ ★ ★

As he approached the city of Schampfanzun some days later, he saw a large cloud of riders coming towards him, and at their head, an elegant figure in brocaded tunic whom he guessed might be his accuser King Vergulaht himself.

'Gawain?' asked the latter as they drew up facing each other, 'well then, though the contest will be deadly, be sure that until then you shall be treated as would the most welcome guest. I must be at the hunt, but my sister will receive you, and when you've seen her, I know that you'll wish me to be a long while away!'

So when Gawain came under the arches of Schampfanzun, he was welcomed in the courtyard by

Antikonie, as shapely as she was lavish in manner, and very clearly pleased by what she saw of her guest.

She ushered him inside, to the room where she'd been sitting with her friends, 'You can be sure,' she promised with a smile of playful wickedness, 'that whatever takes your fancy here can be yours. We could start with a kiss...' The kiss which followed was no modest peck of greeting. Each of her friends now remembered some urgent matter elsewhere. Very soon the two were alone and thoroughly occupied in the hungry stroking of each other's thighs. Just as their last threads of restraint fell away, an old palace official rushed in upon them with some trivial errand. He stared in long-robed horror for an instant and then turned and tore out calling,

'To arms! The man who murdered our old King is raping my lady!'

More shouts echoed around the walls, then clattering and running feet in several directions.

'They've raised the alarm,' the young woman wailed, 'that buffoon has got it all wrong. Hurry! To the tower nearby before they kill you!' But they'd only reached the top of the steps leading to the tower door, when a great ferocious gaggle of townsfolk and men-at-arms swept towards them. With the strength of the cornered, Gawain wrenched from the tower door a long iron bolt, and swung it to and fro as his companion rushed inside to find weapons. She seized the only thing she saw, a large chess set, and ran out thrusting the board at Gawain for a shield – for it had an iron ring at its centre – while she hurled chess pieces at the attackers, her arm strong and aim deadly such that first one, then another, then more, fell to the ground. The sight of her lithe form moving with such vigour next to him well recharged Gawain's own fire and strength.

When Vergulaht the King arrived on the scene, he saw his chance to finish Gawain with ease, and was just unsheathing his sword to join the mob when Kingrimursel his champion also ran up. This was the man who had brought the challenge to Arthur's forest camp.

'This is shameful.' was his first thought, 'my words brought this man here for single combat, but now he's set upon by a mob. My word is at stake!' And drawing his sword, he ran along the wall and sprang to Gawain's side. At this sight, many of the attackers became confused and lowered their weapons.

'What are your orders, Lord?' cried one to Vergulaht,
'Call a truce!' yelled another.
'Someone has to sort this out!' complained a third.

'Lower your weapons!' called out Vergulaht and the shouts subsided.

Then Antikonie's voice rang out. 'You made this man my guest,' she accused her brother, 'and for receiving the hospitality you offered, he was set upon by this pack of animals!'

'At your bidding,' echoed Kingrimursel, 'I challenged this man to come here in good faith. The only way I can make amends to him now is to stand by him.'

Vergulaht, aware that his recent deeds did not reflect well, became the soul of moderation. 'I must withdraw and consult my advisors, as to how this matter might be brought to a satisfactory conclusion. I urge you all,' he nodded at Gawain, 'to recover in comfort whilst I do so.'

Seated in a separate chamber with his friends, Vergulaht
asked them,
'How can I regain the affections of my sister and
Kingrimursel, and yet gain some repayment for the
crime Gawain committed?'

'You told us,' said one, 'how a week ago you were
unhorsed by a Red Knight who then demanded you
discover for him the whereabouts of the Grail. Demand
then, that Gawain agrees to take on this task as well as you.'

All were reassembled in the council room and Gawain
heard the proposal.
'Let everyone hear me say,' he declared, 'that I know
nothing of the original crime, the slaying of the King's
father, but as a way of settling all these quarrels, I agree
to attempt to find the Grail, just as Vergulaht will.'

In the morning, glowing still from the last kiss from the
eager lips of Antikonie, Gawain took to the road. It was
weeks later that Vergulaht learned the true name of his
father's murderer. By that time Gawain was beyond reach
and no one could recall exactly who had first accused him.

★ ★ ★ ★ ★

Later that day his path wound down from crags towards
a glade where a man lay in broken armour, pale, faint
and bleeding. His head was pillowed in the lap of a
whimpering woman. Hurrying over, Gawain knelt and
examined the injured man.

'Blood from the gash in his chest is pressing down on his
heart,' he muttered. Urgently he pulled a strip of bark
from a linden tree and rolled it into a tube. One end he
inserted into the wound and then carefully sucked blood

out. As the man began to breathe more easily, he passed the tube to the woman.

'Which way did your enemy take?' asked Gawain.

'That one,' groaned the other knight, 'but I urge you not to take it. Misery is all you'll earn!' Gawain, though, was already mounting to leave.

Soon his ears picked up the sound of lute and tambourine drifting on the breeze. Then he saw a troupe of dancers, male and female in their full bloom. They seemed lost in gleeful contemplation of each other, a display of fine legs, swirling hair, swaying hips and nimble paces. Gawain longed to be among them. But at his approach they stopped, their carefree faces suddenly anxious.

'Don't go on,' a man no more than twenty said to Gawain as he stepped forward. 'Our Duchess is ahead – at the spring which she tends. But for a knight to encounter her leads to nothing but sorrow. I beg you, for your own safety, to turn back.'

'I can at least see this terrifying woman before I flee her!' smiled Gawain, and rode on, though the warning on their faces looked real enough.

Soon he found himself surrounded by lush groves of olive, fig, pomegranate and vine. He came to a sparkling spring in their midst, and by it stood a woman so lustrous that Gawain would have moaned with desire, were not that ill-bred behaviour to display in a public place towards a stranger.

Instead, with a tone of the most wholehearted admiration in his voice, he said,

'You'd make me the gladdest of men if you'd agree to my joining you there. For certainly I see before me the most glorious of women!'

'Actually,' came the reply, 'I can easily do without tedious compliments from tiresome strangers. If you fancy more insults, and if you like being completely ignored, then follow me.' And she nimbly mounted her horse, as if to put distance between them.

'Such would be a small price to pay,' Gawain persisted, now even more smitten than before, 'if I could at least still seek your affection.' And so he followed her.

Behind him, he heard the faltering hoof-fall of a lame horse. He turned to see a skeletal animal carrying a small round figure, expensively dressed in the blue and gold costume of a page. But this page's hair stood up in bristles like a hedgehog's and on either side of his mouth grew tusk-like teeth very similar to those of Cundrie, the Sorceress. Rightly so, for he was her brother, named Malcreature, as well as servant to Gawain's new companion.

'Well my fine numbskull!' yelled this rider at the knight, 'you must be wanting a tumble and a beating and a very tender backside, if you're trying to pursue my lady Orgeluse.'

Now Gawain's patience snapped.

'I'm not in the habit,' he hissed, 'of receiving such things.' He leaned over from his saddle and reached out vengefully towards the other, 'nor such words from the likes of you!'

He made to grab the rider by the hair and pull him down. The ill-shaped youth cringed and yelped in dismay, then Gawain winced and flinched away as the hedgehog bristles sliced the flesh of his hand.

'Don't, I beg you,' came the bored voice of Orgeluse, 'stop your lively discussion. It's truly entertaining.'

They now arrived back at the clearing where the wounded knight still lay with his nurse tending him. Instantly he tried to rise and stabbed his finger venomously at Orgeluse. 'She's the cause of all my suffering,' he yelled, 'don't have anything to do with her!'

Still struggling to be gracious, Gawain asked,

'Is there some way I can assist you further?' The fallen knight's eyes seemed to cloud with weakness.

'Perhaps,' he faltered, 'you could help my friend there mount her horse and then perhaps help me up behind her...'

'Well certainly,' said Gawain. Then he untied the horse of the fallen knight's companion and beckoned to her. When she stepped over, he lifted her carefully up into the saddle, and at that instant, the knight seemed to be filled with sudden strength, for he leapt to his feet and sprang onto the back of Gawain's own horse, the cherished Gringolet. With a scornful bray, the knight and his companion sped away, leaving Gawain tricked, misused and forlorn.

Only when Gawain heard that bray had he recognised the face of Urian, who had once been sentenced to death at the Court of Arthur for the crime of rape. When Gawain had argued that this sentence was too savage, it had been reduced. Instead, for a month, Urian had been fed with the dogs. The theft of Gringolet was his repayment.

'You make a fine pageboy!' taunted Orgeluse sourly. She turned to her real page: 'Leave him your horse then,' she commanded Cundrie's kin, 'while you make for home.'

Gawain though, remained determined to prove his devotion. He now followed her, leading the knock-kneed and sparse-coated wreck of a horse, coaxing it to keep up, for it was clearly too weak to carry his weight. Maybe an hour passed thus, until the woods gave way to a green sweep of turf, leading to a full-flowing river and beyond it a high-walled castle sprouting many towers. At every window women sat, in ones, twos and threes, their robes fluttering in the breeze. A ferryman, grave-eyed, but kindly, was just pushing off towards the two newcomers from the further shore. And on the far side of the levelled turf, a knight, well-mounted and boldly decked out in black and purple, was just making ready to charge.

'Let's hope,' sneered Orgeluse at Gawain, 'that when he sends you toppling, your breeches split wide and every woman up on those walls has a good view.' Next she stepped into the ferryman's boat and gestured for him to push it away.

As the other knight thundered towards him, Gawain mounted his useless horse, fully aware that a charge was beyond its power. 'My only hope,' he thought, 'is that his horse will stumble as it tramples mine into the ground.'

Indeed, Gawain's opponent lammed into him, but as his horse went down the stranger's mount floundered upon it and in a flurry of flying hooves, lances, shields and tumbling riders, they all crashed to the ground. The two men then clambered to their feet and went hard at each other with their swords. Both swung vigorously and evaded nimbly, and then the same again and again, until the sword arm of each ached painfully. Then a false step sent the other stumbling backwards on the ground and Gawain's sword was at his throat.

'I've never surrendered,' panted the fallen man, 'and I will not do so now.'

But Gawain could not bring himself to strike the death blow at one who had fought with such flare.

'I salute a foe worth fighting!' he said, 'whether or not you surrender, I will not strike to kill...'

He turned away, leaving the other battered and unable to rise from the ground, and went up to examine the horse which by rights he had now won. Much of its form and colouring were covered by jousting colours. He led it to a rock and mounted, then found something very familiar in the spring of its stride, the arch of its neck.

'Gringolet!' he sighed, recognising the cherished mount of which he had been cheated so recently and which seemed in so short a time to have passed to another, then back to him.

He was fondly caressing the hefty flank, when he heard the lapping of water against wood, and saw the ferryman returning. Onto the boat he led Gringolet, leaving the other man still winded on the ground.

'What castle is this?' he asked the boatman.

'Don't ask that. Whatever battles you may have known, they are like a game of marbles compared with what lies within those walls. The knight I ferried yesterday was sensible and kept his mouth shut the whole time. You may know him, he wore red armour.'

'I know him,' smiled Gawain, 'but I'll go into the castle anyway, so you may as well tell me.'

'You have no idea what you're saying! This is the castle of Clinschor the Sorcerer, and all those ladies are held there by his craft. When he was young, he was devoted to all the exploits of knighthood. Until he was discovered in the bed of the Queen of Sicily by the King of Sicily. The raging King then swung his sword to clip Clinschor's male parts. The only balm for Clinschor's wounded soul was to become a master of the occult arts. He studied magic wherever its teachers could be found and this castle is one of his devices. If any knight survived its halls, he would become Lord of the castle. But it is not possible to do so.'

'That's the very reason I must attempt it.'

'If I cannot dissuade you,' sighed the ferryman, 'do one thing first. Your shield is now torn and bent. I have many at my house left over from fights at this spot. Take a fresh one from there.'

So it was with an undamaged shield that Gawain stepped through the castle gates and cautiously entered the great hall. It was empty, but in the far wall stood a heavy door. This he shoved open to find a small chamber containing a great bed. When he stepped towards it, it moved away. He could see that the wheels on which it stood were made of ruby, but the force that propelled it was invisible. When he went to one side, it moved to the other. When he went to the other, it moved back. This filled Gawain with a mighty urge to lie upon it. So he took a couple of steps and a great leap and landed squarely in the middle. From that moment, the bed slammed from wall to wall, as if frenzied, so that he could not get upright enough to have hope of getting off. Now a grave premonition came over him. He instantly gathered in his legs, arms and head and pulled the shield to cover as much of him as he could, like a tortoise in mortal danger.

Hardly had he done so than from every direction a hail of stones and metal rained down on him. First came the bolts of innumerable slingshots, mauling shield and armour with an ear-dulling clatter. No sooner had the sound subsided, than as many vicious arrows whirred through the air towards him. Every inch of the bed was pierced, but it had stopped moving. It took Gawain some moments to convince himself that, though he was battered and sliced where the shield had been pierced, he had managed to survive beneath it.

As, with difficulty, he dragged himself from the bed, he felt tremors, then heard a sound like enraged roaring. Into the room, snarling murderously, slunk a creature with lion-like appearance, but the size of a horse. For what felt like an age, the two circled, taking swipes at each other, until with one desperate, but well-timed lunge, Gawain hacked a leg from the beast. In a hurricane of pain and fury, the creature took one great leap at the man who, as he fell under the massive body onto the blood-soaked floor, plunged his sword upwards. It was a lifeless weight that crashed to the ground covering him.

As he wriggled out breathless and nearly senseless from under it, the door opened. As he lay on the ground he looked up into a circle of anxious women's faces. Dimly, as he lost consciousness, he recognised his own sister, Itonje, among them. Under the supervision of the eldest, a matron whom the others clearly held in high regard, they brought herbs, dressings and salves to tend his many wounds, and these they began to administer with utmost care. In a nearby room a log fire was kindled and a soft bed was made. Into this Gawain was lifted and the older woman placed under his tongue one leaf of a sleep-inducing herb.

★ ★ ★ ★ ★

In spite of the skilful attentions of the women, Gawain's night was troubled. His bandaged body writhed, his mind was tormented by lush and tantalising visions of Orgeluse. Still weak and dazed when he arose the next day, he wandered hesitantly through the sorcerer's chambers.

He came towards a great pillar with an intricate woodland scene painted upon it, or so it seemed. For the figures in that scene suddenly twitched and scurried. As, with heart racing, he came a little closer, they continued to move, and he seemed to recognise the groves and wastes around the castle, somehow shown upon the pillar's surface. He found that he was watching riders approach the walls, and was then even more startled to recognise the haughty and entrancing face of Orgeluse. An unknown knight accompanied her devotedly.

'The pillar shows all that is happening in the country around us,' came a voice behind him, and he turned to see the face of Arnive, the mother of Arthur himself, who had been among those held in the castle and had overseen his nursing, 'it is one of Clinschor's sorceries.'

'Then help me arm, I beg you!' said Gawain, 'for one comes whom I must meet!'

'But your injuries have hardly begun to mend', came the voice of his sister Itonje who had also come upon them as they talked. He hardly seemed to hear.

'I must go,' came his reply, 'I depend on you to help me get ready.' He lurched to his bedroom and his armour, their pleading falling on deaf ears.

It wasn't long afterwards that Orgeluse's new companion lay bruised and breathless on the ground before Gawain.

'So you've won another fight!' sniffed the Duchess, 'so you've even survived the Bed of Terrors! But if you knew what you'd have to do to earn a fond glance from me, even you would begin to quail.'

'If that were the prize,' came the answer, 'there's nothing I would not attempt.'

'I wonder how long such brave words will last. You see, on the other side of that ravine, a tree. You must get from it a sprig of leaves. But it is guarded by Gramoflanz, a fighter so deadly that he never bothers to face less than two foes at once. Once he brought me misery.'

'How so?'

'He slew my husband. He held me against my will, trying to make me give in to him.'

'So be it,' said Gawain grim-faced, for the ravine was wide, its edges of crumbling rock. He urged Gringolet into a big-hearted canter. The horse leapt and stretched wide. Its front hooves landed on the far edge, but its rear hooves scrabbled to gain a hold on the loose surface. Stones fell away into the chasm and straight after, the horse and rider followed them. Down they plummeted, towards the rushing torrent at the bottom. Gawain splashed into the deeps, but within reach of the shore. He struggled up onto it with the water gushing from his steel plates. But Gringolet flailed helplessly in the grip of a ravenous whirlpool. Now Gawain leaned towards the rushing water with his lance, and hooked the reins with the tip. Digging in his heels and straining, he now managed to haul the treasured horse against the pull of the water towards the bank. Then Gringolet found his footing.

When Gawain had recovered his breath and Gringolet had given a great shake to send the water showering from his coat, the two of them, side by side, scrambled and zig-zagged up the far wall of the chasm. They reached the tree, which seemed unguarded. Gawain scoured his surroundings with his eyes, then wrenched off a cluster of leaves. But as soon as he thrust this into the band round his helmet, a horseman burst from the bushes.

'That garland has not been won yet!' he barked. 'But as you can see,' he went on, quietening, 'I am unarmed at the moment, and by the look of you and the state of your shield, I'd say you were far from fresh. Meet me instead in sixteen days, and let us ask all comers to attend.'

'Nothing,' said Gawain, 'would please me more!'

'But,' the other continued, 'I also request a favour from you. Though we meet as foes, yet I estimate you a man of generosity enough to grant it.'

'You may be my enemy, but I also read signs of merit in your bearing,' replied Gawain, 'so ask!'

'Do you know the maiden called Itonje?'

'I do.'

'She is the sister of the man I count as my deadliest enemy, Gawain, whose father killed my own father. She and I have never met face to face. Yet she is the one for whom I long. Take her, I beg you, my ring and my pledge of service.'

'I will readily do this,' came the answer, 'such are the signs of worth I see in you, even though I am that Gawain of whom you speak.'

Confusion, regret and delight all flickered in the eyes of Gramoflanz. 'Then I give you my heartfelt thanks now,' he concluded, 'as I will give all my strength against you in sixteen days.'

Gawain headed Gringolet at the chasm once more, and this time the big-hearted horse landed squarely upon the far side. When he trotted up to the place where Orgeluse still waited, and dismounted, she threw herself at his feet with tears pouring from her eyes. Gawain was utterly at a loss as to how to respond to this sudden and complete reversal.

'However much you want me,' she wailed, 'it's not worth putting yourself in such danger.'

'But... I thought...'

'I wasn't going to consider any man, unless he was up to the task of facing Gramoflanz, and I never thought I'd find one. But now I have, I don't want to lose him. And anyway,' her face dissolved into tears once more, 'I haven't wanted to lose you from the first moment we met.'

Scarcely believing this happy turn of events, Gawain gently clasped her shoulders. 'Perhaps,' he smiled, 'a kiss is now in order.'

'And more,' replied Orgeluse meltingly, 'but I don't much like holding all this armour in my arms. Come back with me to my lands, and there you may remove it in safety.'

IV: King

The glades resounded with the sound of metal striking metal. Parsifal and a knight from the East were locked in struggle. Then Parsifal brought Anfortas' sword down upon his foe's collarbone. At which moment, the blade shattered like an earthenware pot. For an instant, his foe was as startled as he, long enough for Parsifal to hurl his shield at the other's head and send him toppling from the saddle. Even that fight he did not lose.

But afterwards, just as Sigune had once instructed him, he sought out the place where, in a far corner of the woods, guarded by ferns and mosses, the spring at Karnant flowed.

Before first light he placed the pieces under the gushing water, saw a sparkle and a kind of wiggling there, and pulled out the sword rejoined, now far stronger than before.

'If only my heart could be mended so well', he sighed, and rode on.

With a twisting trail of further battles behind him, Parsifal came to a shadowy place deep among the trees, where a brook flowed. Bridging the water, stood a sturdy hut. Hearing the soft thud of slow-moving hooves, the hermit who sheltered there came out to meet the visitor. Parsifal now saw that it was a woman in a grey robe, but with a garnet ring upon her finger and a band in her hair which signified widowhood.

'How can you survive here,' he asked wonderingly, 'so far from anywhere else?'

'My food comes straight from the Grail,' answered the other, 'Cundrie the Sorceress brings it to me once every week.'

Parsifal's pulse quickened at word of the Grail. 'And are you all alone here?' he persisted.

'Never,' she answered, 'my beloved is always with me.' She gestured then towards the open door of her hut and Parsifal only now made out the long dark shape within. It was a coffin. And only now did he realise that once more he looked upon Sigune, still attending her dead beloved, just as she also recognised him.

'It's you,' she whispered, 'whom I named. And whom I cursed, when you came from your tongue-tied visit to the Fisher King. But I can see, looking at you now, that what you did there has caused you as much pain as anyone. This I can read in your eyes. No longer would I spit in your face. Hurry now, Cundrie only just left here after she brought my weekly food. You can follow the tracks of her mule, and they could lead you back to the Grail Castle. Maybe there's a second chance, even for you.'

She showed him where the hoofprints of Cundrie's mule led away from the clearing. He followed this winding trail a mile or more. It led him to a place of towering rocks, gullies, and half-hidden by the boughs of a chestnut tree – a menacing figure. A rider, his well-muscled horse pitch black, his costly trappings and weapons adorned with white turtledoves.

'You trespass!' he accused Parsifal, 'only those who serve the Grail can venture here.' Then he couched his lance.

The two thundered at each other along the edge of a gorge. When they met, Parsifal's aim was the truer, and

56

the Grail knight was hurled out of his saddle and into the chasm. But Parsifal's horse, unable to stop in time, also careered over the edge as its rider frantically grasped the branches of a small tree gripping the rocks. As he struggled back onto firm ground he could see the other man far below, picking himself up painfully and limping away. And he could see the motionless form of his red horse, once so proud, willing and sure-footed.

Then his eyes fell upon the black horse nosing the scrub a few yards away, its reins trailing the ground. So he mounted from a tree stump and rode off, now bearing the turtledove emblem of the Grail. Cundrie's track began to get faint, but he followed it still, often having to search for it among the rotted leaves and roots. Then it petered out, and he was as lost as ever.

★ ★ ★ ★ ★

When many more months had passed, there came a day when the sprouting green of springtime again lay in the grip of an untimely snowfall, as it had once at the camp of Arthur. As he rode, Parsifal thought,

'No-one could be more lost than I. I have been deserted by God. I could have won my way to the Grail, but I failed. I have the dearest of wives, but I cannot return to her while I am so worthless. I can only let my reins fall from my hands. If God is anything but cruel and heartless – which I doubt – then **He** can guide my horse to wherever I should go.'

When, soon after, the surroundings became faintly familiar, this in no way cheered him. From a cave beneath the cliff ahead of him emerged the hermit Trevrizent, whom he had first met that day he clashed with Orilus and relieved Jeschute of her misery.

'How heavy your misfortunes must be,' said the older man to the newcomer, 'that you must ride out armed on Good Friday.'

'I didn't know it was that day,' Parsifal replied grimly, 'but it would make no difference if I did. For God has abandoned me. I could have won the Grail, but failed. I have the dearest of wives, but I cannot return to her while I am so cast down.'

'Who are you?'

'I am the son of Gahmuret.'

'Then I am your uncle,' gasped the old man, 'your mother was my sister. Do you yet know that she died as soon as you left her?'

Parsifal reeled back as if pierced by a blade.
'I did not, but this news only tells me how right I am to despise myself.' His uncle, though, shook his head and spoke soothingly. 'By spending much time in prayer, I have come to know God better than many. I assure you that He never entirely abandons anyone, even if He sometimes reflects back to them what they give out, like a mirror. You may also not know that Ither, the Red Knight you killed, was your relative. But neither would that cause God to desert you. As to this matter of the Grail, you should trouble yourself about it no more. The great gemstone has written upon its sides the names of all the men and women called to serve it. They find their way there without hindrance. When a land is without a king or queen, then one of their number goes out to take up that crown. But if your name is not there, the matter is closed and there is no need to upset yourself with it.'

Trevrizent led the way into his cave, where a fire crackled and flared, easing the stiffness in the young man's limbs.

'Let me tell you more of the Grail', he continued, 'for I once lived at that castle, called 'Munsalvaesche', or 'Wild Mountain'. Not only does any vessel brought before the gemstone become filled with food or drink, but any person sick or injured who is brought before it is filled with strength, and shall live for a further week at least, however severe their plight. This shall continue as long as they view the jewel. It was brought to earth by riders from beyond the stars. Once there was a war between the Angels of Light and those of Darkness. A third group of Angels took neither side, and the riders were those Angels, who left the Grail behind them on Earth when they returned to the heavens. Today, as on every Good Friday, a white dove glides down from above with a morsel of bread in its beak. This it places upon the jewel before flapping its way skywards again. This seems to renew the power of the Grail.

'My brother Anfortas is the Grail King. Anyone who attains that office must give up all intimacy with women. Except that is, within marriage. But my brother yearned for a certain beauty, Orgeluse, and jousted in her name. In one such joust, the point of his enemy's spear pierced his testicle, and he was carried from the field in torment. This wound has never healed, the pain never leaves him. He would die of it, but every night the Grail is brought before him, and so he lives on in agony. He can neither sit nor lie, walk nor ride. Some say the spear was the very same which pierced the side of the Christ. My brother is sometimes called the Fisher King because he often spends time upon the lake waters, which seems to soothe his pain, and freshens the air about him.

'Once, words appeared upon the sides of the gemstone, saying
'A stranger knight will come, and he will ask the question which will end the suffering of the Grail King.' Soon after, one did arrive, but, heartlessly, he asked no question, and so left the Grail Fellowship in deeper sorrow than he found them.'

'Uncle,' said the young man, his voice grave, 'that stranger knight was me.'

'What a dismal fate!' gasped his uncle. And for some moments it seemed that even he, so sure of God's goodwill, saw the young man's plight as hopeless. Then he spoke again,

'I will speak with God in my prayers and I will make this offer. If your own actions do not make sufficient amends for what you have done, then I will pay whatever price is required, whatever pain or hardship it may mean.'

'Uncle,' responded Parsifal, 'that is generosity beyond anything I've ever known. To know that you'd be willing to do it is enough.'

Heartened by his uncle's words, Parsifal bade him farewell. His black horse moved at a steady walk, carrying its head low as if also contemplating the meaning of the old man's words.

★ ★ ★ ★ ★

A vast camp is pitched once more amidst the oak and the alders, for many have come to witness the great duel between Gawain and Gramoflanz. Arthur and his folk are there and all the people of Orgeluse, as well as the friends, relatives and supporters of Gramoflanz.

Before any of the sleepers in the tents around him stir, Gawain arises and rides down to the jousting ground for practice. He struggles to ignore the weakness and weariness which come from his recent ordeals in the Castle of Clinschor and the chasm nearby. But he finds his foe has risen even earlier and seems to be waiting for him. He sees that Gramoflanz, to identify himself, wears in his helmet a garland of leaves from the tree he usually guards.

Lumps of turf fly high in the air as they hurtle towards each other, meeting in a grim deadlock like two stags with their antlers caught, such that both horses crash to the ground. The spilled riders clamber to their feet and soon the air is ringing with the sound of sword on shield. As the breath is knocked from his body again and again, Gawain knows all too well that he's never known such a foe.

A pair of messengers is just passing between the camps and comes upon the struggle.

'Gawain!' one of them yells in alarm. 'What are you doing?' A dismayed cry of

'NO!' then rings out from beneath the helmet of Gawain's attacker. He lurches back, drops his sword and tugs off his helmet. Gawain sags onto his knees with exhaustion as he looks up into the face of Parsifal. The latter had drifted that way upon his twisting journey, having first plucked leaves from the tree of Gramoflanz. This, he had been told by foresters, would earn him a formidable foe, and so it had seemed to turn out. Now Gramoflanz himself rode up, eyeing the badly-mauled Gawain with vexation.

'Gawain,' he fussed, 'is in no condition to fight me now! This has spoilt everything!'

'I can assure you,' answered his opponent, 'that by tomorrow I'll again be quite ready to face you.' But Parsifal was viewing Gawain carefully and could see upon him the marks of his many recent trials. He could tell without doubt that it would take far more than one night's rest to restore him to full strength. Gawain, he knew, was likely to die if he fought.

When Arthur, Gawain and all their companions were still at Mass next morning, Gramoflanz rode out ready on the dewy turf. As the others approached the jousting ground later, they heard the ring of steel on steel, and exchanged perplexed glances. Arriving, they found Gramoflanz hard-pressed by some enemy clad in Gawain's surcoat, emblazoned with its five-pointed star. Arthur and Gawain shot forward, others close behind.

'Stop this at once!' roared the king.

'How,' cried Gramoflanz as he lowered his sword and looked disbelieving at the rider next to Arthur, 'can Gawain be *there*,' he pointed now at the foe before him, '... and *there*?'

But Gawain himself nodded sagely,

'My friend, Parsifal,' he said, 'has tried to make the odds between us even, by tiring you out, as I was worn out by yesterday's fight and many before. But I cannot have it said that I fought a man already weakened by another. Our joust shall take place tomorrow.'

It was only now that, as Arthur sat in his pavilion pondering on these events, Itonje, the sister of Gawain, crept in shyly.

'You must stop this fight,' she begged him, her eyes full of pain, 'if you do not, either my brother will be killed, or else,' and she stared nervously at the floor, 'my beloved will be killed.'

'What is this?' queried Arthur, 'Gramoflanz has offered you his devotion?'

'He has. My brother himself brought the message.'

'And you return it?'

'I do.' And the great King took the tearful young woman comfortingly in his arms.

Soon after, Arthur sent out to the camp of Gramoflanz, calling the knight's uncle to a private meeting in his tent.

'Persuade Gramoflanz,' he urged 'to give up the challenge, for the sake of Itonje.'

The old man returned to the other camp and Arthur sent a messenger to fetch Orgeluse.

'Persuade Gawain, if you can,' he encouraged her, 'to give up the challenge, for the sake of Itonje.' Willingly enough she went off, for by now Gawain's survival meant much more to her than her revenge.

Soon after, all of them were called together on the jousting green, where they listened to consoling words from Arthur. A few moments of awkward silence followed, and then a sudden outbreak of hand-shaking and back-slapping and cheek-kissing and a buzz of merry and relieved voices.

As these sounds of merriment echoed through the trees, Parsifal rode away alone.

★ ★ ★ ★ ★

It was very soon after that he seemed to catch sight of something glinting among the foliage ahead. Then he found himself approaching a warrior fully armed, whose surcoat was studded with sparkling gems, the costliest Parsifal had ever seen. The crest of the man's helmet was fashioned in the likeness of an ecidemon, that creature swift and deadly to all snakes.

They met at speed with a clap and shriek of wood and metal breaking, for each had shattered the other's shield. Then they circled each other, battling until their horses were stumbling with exhaustion. First the stranger, then Parsifal jumped down to continue on foot. Parsifal now discovered he had never met another so fierce and quick. As blow followed blow, for the first time ever he began to sag at the knees. He struggled to brace himself and saw how, for an instant, the other's helm with its ecidemon crest lay unprotected. In that moment he brought his sword hard down upon it. But in the instant that steel touched, the blade shattered into a hundred fragments. Parsifal stood there, paralysed with astonishment. But now his assailant also lowered his weapon.

'It would do me no credit to defeat a man with no sword,' he said from beneath his helm. 'Hold off, and if you will, tell me your name.'

'Yours first,' retaliated Parsifal, as if still locked in combat.

'I am Feirefiz,' the other replied, 'I rule six lands across the sea in Africa, but I am of the bloodline of Anjou.'

'How can you be?' queried Parsifal. 'That's my family. I once did hear strange news of a brother, but you can't be him, can you? CAN YOU... be him!?'

In answer the other removed his helmet, and Parsifal saw the face of Feirefiz with shades of black and white intermingled.

'Your father was Gahmuret?' Parsifal demanded.

'Long ago,' replied the other, 'he came to the land of my mother, Belacane, upon the sands of Africa. He defended her territory and earned her heart. He left there before I was born. I never did understand why. I heard that in all other matters he was a man of merit. Whether it was because his faith forbade him to wed a woman of another faith, I cannot say for certain.'

'Well,' Parsifal commented, 'I never saw him either. That we both share.' A few moments of awe-struck silence followed, and then each clasped the other in his arms.

Before long, Feirefiz sat in the place of honour at Arthur's table, and the wondering Parsifal felt able at last to share some of the jollity of the other revellers. Their voices, though, failed to drown the sound of approaching hoofbeats.

As on that other occasion when well-being had been snatched from Parsifal as he sat with Arthur, a woman rode towards them, though this time on a fine horse rather than a mule. Her gown of dark velvet was covered with golden turtledoves, and her face heavily veiled. But when she halted and lifted the veil, all recognised the boar-tusk teeth and bear-like ears of Cundrie.

'I bring news,' her voice rang clear, 'from the Castle of the Grail. New words have appeared upon the surface of the gemstone. They name the new Grail King. That name is Parsifal.'

'But how could that be?' uttered Parsifal, his voice hushed, eyes wide with confusion. 'My uncle told me that no one ever struggled their way to the Grail. If your name was not already upon it, that was the end of the matter...'

'Nevertheless,' Cundrie answered firmly, 'it has happened. I ask you to come with me now to the castle, and also to choose one companion for the journey.'

'Then' came the answer, without hesitation, 'I choose Feirefiz, my brother from across the seas.' So the two of them rose from their places at the table, and their horses were brought while Arthur's company looked on, their eyes filled with awe.

★ ★ ★ ★ ★

The men and women of the Grail Castle lined its corridors and bowed their heads in welcome as Parsifal and Feirefiz walked down them, towards the place where Anfortas waited. But when they passed the spot where Repanse de Schoye, the Grail bearer, stood among the others, her eyes grew wide and fixed on the face of Feirefiz as if in sudden recognition. Only with effort could she tear them away. Recently Anfortas' pain had risen to new heights. His fur-swaddled body and desperate eyes told the tale of that torment as Parsifal came close.

'As the new Grail King,' pleaded the older man, 'you could end my suffering by ordering them to withhold the Grail from me. Then at least I could die.'

Leaning still closer and looking into the sick man's eyes, Parsifal instead let fall from his lips the words

'Uncle, what ails you?'

The change which came about in Anfortas was at first scarcely perceptible, yet all saw it without mistake. He released a sigh from his heart's depths. There was a slight change in his colouring. Then his soul and body were flooded with well-being.

'Who would ever have thought this could be?' he marvelled as he looked into the tear-filled eyes of all his companions around him.

'Do you yet know,' he asked as he smiled at his nephew, 'that Condwiramurs has also been named as the Grail Queen? We have had ample time to gather news of your exploits and know how it lies between the two of you. She has been sent for and is now only a day's journey away.'

'Then let me go and meet her at once!' cried Parsifal, instantly whirling round to dash off with a small band of followers in train.

So they set out, but on their way turned aside long enough for Parsifal to tell the hermit Trevizent what had occurred.

'Never before,' uttered the old man shaking his head in disbelief, 'has the Grail King been chosen in this way. Never...'

The riders continued their journey through the night, as stars peeped between the leaves above them and the woodland creatures scurried about them. But at dawn they came upon the silent tents of the Queen's company. It was a scene so like that other one years before, with Parsifal pulling back the tent flap, then pausing to look upon all the womanly glory of the sleeping figure. But this time two small and tousled figures lay, one on either side of Condwiramurs. These were the twin boys born in Parsifal's five year absence. And this time he waited, spellbound, until his wife stirred, then looked up. A cry of astonishment escaped her lips, then a sigh of longing, a growl of angry reproach followed by another sigh of longing.

'It's been so very long...' she said.

'But now,' he replied softly, 'it need never be so again.' The two children blinked sleepily, and she called softly to a maidservant, who came, cradled them in her arms and carried them to a neighbouring tent. From that moment the two were unseen by anyone else until mid-morning, but we can be sure they found the sweetest ways to fill that time, locked in each other's arms.

When they had finally emerged, the whole party headed in the direction of the Grail Castle. This time, though, they turned aside to call at the other hermitage, that of Sigune, where it bridged the shadowy brook. Entering the doorway, they found her kneeling deep in prayer. Going closer, they saw that her body had that stillness which only comes with death.

Intending to join her at long last with her beloved, they lifted the lid of his coffin and saw a trim, armoured body and a tranquil face, as fresh as at the moment of his last breath. Carefully they placed the body of Sigune within, and together they left them.

That night as they all feasted in the Castle called 'Wild Mountain', Feirefiz witnessed the stately procession of the young women. It reached its climax with the arrival of a beauty who far eclipsed any he had ever laid eyes upon, the Grail bearer Repanse de Schoye. What she carried, though, appeared to him a mere precious stone, such as many he had seen or possessed. As if a screen hung before his eyes, the moment of filling the empty vessels also remained hidden from him. But the one who carried it – she was another matter entirely.

He turned to the serene Anfortas, his eagerness dispelling all reserve,

'I am disarmed completely by the sight of that incomparable one. What chance have I of earning her affections? How ready might she be to consider marriage?'

Anfortas regarded him consolingly,

'I understand,' he replied, 'that you have far more jewels, wider lands and more fighters at your command than any of our kings, and that Zazamanc teems with artists and craftsmen who make ours look like hamfisted apprentices. It seems the only thing you do not have is Repanse de Schoye. I happen to know that she has already spoken admiringly of you. But as a Grail Maiden, she has promised only to marry another of the same faith.'

'So I would have to adopt hers?' asked the African, 'That would be small hardship for such great reward!'

So a ceremony was arranged. In the temple of the castle stood a font made from one single ruby. Two helpers tilted it towards the Grail and it filled with clear water. A silver-haired priest placed his fingers in the water and then upon the forehead of Feirefiz, saying,

'This betokens belief in three beings which are also one: God the Father, the Son and the Holy Spirit.'

'I am willing to believe in this,' Feirefiz replied, 'if it joins me with Repanse de Schoye.'

When he stepped out of the temple she was waiting to receive him with a kiss long and fond. That night in the banqueting hall, he found that he saw before him not an ordinary gem but the full splendour of the Grail. And he saw that as the serving men brought the vessels before it, they became filled to the brim with the finest food and drink.

Days later, heart-sore to be leaving his brother's land, yet glad to see his beloved riding at his side, he set out for his land of Zazamanc. Parsifal and Condwiramurs remained at Munsalvaesche, now keepers of the great secret – of riches without limit, of vigour without cease, of wisdom without end, and of unbroken love between man and woman. If you, my reader, find this defies understanding and wish to grasp it more fully, then what you must do is this: tell the tale again, yourself, and then tell it again.

Notes of Perfomances & Workshops

KELVIN HALL offers live story tellings of the Parsifal Story, interwoven with songs from the troubadour tradition of the 13th Century sung by Barbara Hall. Many other storytelling programmes are also available, plus workshops on:

1) The Art of Storytelling.

2) Using the Parsifal story to gain perspectives on our individual lives and choices.

For more information contact:

Kelvin Hall
at Cherry Tree Cottage, Shortwood, Nailsworth,
Gloucestershire, GL6 0SB, England.

Other Books from Hawthorn Press

Told by the Peat Fire
Sibylle Alexander

The voice behind these much loved Celtic tales is the passionate voice of a true storyteller – it crackles with humour and ancient wisdom as it lifts the veil between us and the spiritual world.

Today's revival of the art of storytelling is a sign that people remember the rich and splendid heritage of the past, and are discovering fresh inspiration to create new stories. Sibylle Alexander is a midwife to the imagination; bringing ancient and timeless tales to ears and eyes alike.

These are universal stories of power and laughter offering as much hope and reassurance to the listeners of today as they did through the long nights of winters past.

At the heart of these wonderful stories is the passion of a true storyteller. Sibylle Alexander has the gift, the energy and the vivid imagination to make the words of her tales sing.
Dr Donald Smith,
Director of the Scottish Storytelling Centre

I just loved the stories you sent me. I gobbled them all up and now I am digesting them one by one. I wept over some of them. I was very sad over others. Each one of them seemed to touch the strings of my heart. I hope I can keep them and share them with others.
Eileen Caddy,
Findhorn Foundation

128pp; 216 x 138 mm; 1 869 890 23 X; pb

The Green Snake and the Beautiful Lily

Play Version – Michael Burton
Original Translation of the Fairy Tale –
Thomas Carlyle
The Art of Goethean Conversation –
Marjorie Spock
Johann Wolfgang von Goethe
A group of people live in a world turned
upside down. They realise that the
efforts of one alone can do little to
create a new society. But by waking up to each other at the
right time, they bring about profound spiritual and social
renewal. Goethe originally told this magic tale in a group of
travellers during the French Revolution. Today, this magic still
sparkles in Thomas Carlyle's original translation.

*'This inspiring script is a genuine contribution, combining the grace
of the original fairy tale with a brilliant use of the modern idiom'*
Jay Ramsay

208 pp; 270 x 210mm; illustrations; 1 869 890 85 X; pb

New Eyes for Plants

A workbook for observing and
drawing plants
*Margaret Colquhoun and
Axel Ewald*
Simple observation exercises interwoven with inspiring illustrations
to take you on a vivid journey
through the seasons with a fresh
pair of eyes. Using the holistic
approach of Goethe, this book
opens a door 'onto a new way of
practising Science as an Art'.
208 pp; 270 x 210mm; illustrations; 1 869 890 85 X; pb

Drawing and Painting in Rudolf Steiner Schools

Margrit Jünemann and
Fritz Weitmann

This comprehensive account of painting and drawing in the Steiner curriculum is an invaluable resource book – for all teachers of art as well as for anyone interested in the creative development of children.

It shows how artistic and intellectual activities are fully integrated in order to lead children through the many fascinating and challenging stages of their voyage toward adulthood. It combines detailed practical advice with clearly defined philosophy on aesthetic education.

206 pp; 240 x 170mm; illustrations; 1 869 890 41 8; pb

70 Years A-Growing

Jean Westlake

This book is the story of a magical life committed to organic and bio-dynamic gardening, and has been 70 years in the making.

Packed with practical gardening information, it is also an enticing autobiography. It follows the twists and turns of the Westlake family from developing the famous New Forest holiday centre at Sandy Balls, Fordingbridge to the accolade of having their produce recognised by The Soil Association.

Full of delicious humour, intriguing stories, and written in the wider context of a fascinating life, it will leave you feeling like a member of the family – desperate to return home and catch up with old friends.

256pp; 246 x 189mm; 1 869 890 37 X; pb

Gardening for Life – The Biodynamic Way

A practical introduction to a new art of gardening, sowing, planting, harvesting

Maria Thun

Biodynamic techniques recognise that plant life is intimately bound up with the life of the soil; that the soil itself is alive and vital and that the degree of vitality has a direct bearing on the health of the crops. Through the nurture and care of the soil you will soon be able to grow quality produce which possesses vitality and has the highest flavour.

Sharing its principles, methods and techniques with organic farming, biodynamic agriculture additionally acknowledges that the plant's growth is also affected by planetary influences like the waxing and waning of the moon.

Whether you are an experienced gardener or not, whether or not you have used permaculture or grown organic produce before, this book offers accessible tips on: favourable times for planting, harvesting and growing; ways of combating pests and diseases; building soil fertility – crop changes and rotation; how planets and stars affect plant growth.

This beautifully illustrated, comprehensive guide is a must for all thoughtful gardeners wishing to work in harmony with heaven and earth.
Jean Westlake,
gardener and author

128pp; 212 x 160mm; 1 869 890 32 9; pb

Naming

Choosing a meaningful name
Caroline Sherwood
Names matter. They are the fingerprints of the Soul through which we express our nature to the world. Choosing a meaningful name is a lifetime gift.

Included in this thorough, authoritative, and fascinating book is everything you need to choose, or change, a name and plan a naming ceremony.

Including: what to take into account when choosing a name; the cultural importance of names; meanings to names – a comprehensive dictionary; naming ceremonies to choose from; holding your own ceremony; taking a new name.

Rosie Styles, of The Baby Naming Society, has written the Foreword for this extensive and insightful book, and says;
... Caroline Sherwood's Naming *is a completely new and far more useful approach in which the meanings of names are the prime focus. With a deep respect for language, she offers a fresh way for parents to set about finding the right name for their child. This is a much needed addition to the naming books already available, and will delight anyone facing the enormous task of naming their child, or those with an interest in names.*

A true name offers a bridge between 'you' and 'me'. We should be glad of such a book which shows a way beyond labelling towards a naming of essence and potential in the children who come to us.
Paul Matthews,
author of *Sing Me the Creation*

304pp; 246 x 189mm; 1 869 890 56 6; pb

Tapestries

Weaving life's journey
Betty Staley

Tapestries gives a moving and wise guide to women's life phases. Drawing on original biographies of a wide variety of women, informed by personal experience and by her understanding of anthroposophy, Betty Staley offers a vivid account of life journeys. This book helps readers reflect on their own lives and prepare for the next step in weaving their own biographical tapestry.

336pp; 216 x 138mm; 1 869 890 15 9; pb

Soul Weaving

How to shape your destiny and inspire your dreams

Betty Staley

Soul Weaving is an invitation to weave a design for the Soul's journey bringing together the colours and textures of our personality to reveal pattern and meaning. *Soul Weaving* is the most comprehensive introduction to the temperaments, archetypes and soul qualities, as defined by Rudolf Steiner, which enable us to better understand ourselves and our relationship to the world.

This book shows us how to: transform our temperament; realise and integrate our soul type; understand the influences of the archetypal points of view; make life changes such as choosing a spiritual path, living in balance, cultivating the power of love, and much more.

240pp; 216 x 138mm; 1 869 890 05 1; pb

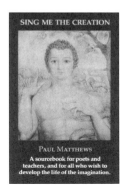

Sing Me the Creation
Paul Matthews

This is an inspirational workbook of creative writing exercises for poets and teachers, and for all who wish to develop the life of the imagination. There are over 300 exercises for improving writing skills. Though intended for group work with adults, teachers will find these exercises easily adaptable to the classroom.

224pp; 238 x 135mm; 1 869 890 60 4; pb

If you have difficulties ordering Hawthorn Press books from a bookshop, you can order direct from:

Scottish Book Source Distribution, 137 Dundee Street, Edinburgh, EH11 1BG.

Tel: 0131 229 6800 Fax: 0131 229 9070